James Cook

IN SEARCH OF

TERRA

INCOGNITA

The Virginia Commonwealth University Series
for Contemporary Poetry

Walton Beacham, General Editor

Moving Out,
by David Walker, 1976

The Ventriloquist,
by Robert Huff, 1977

Rites of Strangers
by Phyllis Janowitz, 1978

James Cook

IN SEARCH OF

TERRA

INCOGNITA

A Book of Poems

———•••———

Jeanne Larsen

University Press of Virginia

Charlottesville

THE UNIVERSITY PRESS OF VIRGINIA
Copyright © 1979 by the Rector and Visitors
of the University of Virginia

First Published 1979

Library of Congress Cataloging in Publication Data

Larsen, Jeanne.
James Cook in search of terra incognita.

(The Virginia Commonwealth University series for contemporary poetry)
I. Title. II. Series: Virginia Commonwealth University. Virginia Commonwealth University series for contemporary poetry.
PS3562.A735J3   811'.5'4   79–20761   ISBN 0–8139–0849–3

"Turning the Edge" first appeared in the *Virginia Quarterly Review* 49, no. 2 (Spring 1973), copyright © 1973 by The Virginia Quarterly Review.

Unavnuk's song, quoted in Part 1 of "Alchemist's Notebook," is from *The Book of the Eskimos*, by Peter Freuchen, copyright © 1961 by Peter Freuchen, and is reprinted by permission of the Harold Matson Company, Inc.

Printed in the United States of America

Contents

6   *Contents*

1
Learning the Land

———◆•◆———

The rocks, the air, everything speaking with audible voice or silent: joyful, wonderful, enchanting, banishing weariness and sense of time. No longing for anything now or hereafter as we go home into the mountain's heart.
—*John Muir*

Nor have I ascended into heaven, nor have I seen all the works and creations of God, but heaven has revealed itself within my spirit in such a way that I there recognize the divine works and creations.
—*Jakob Böhme*

When the Wind

When the wind
the wind blows
we are
when the wind blows
a breath. When
the wind blows and the sun's
up like a sigh
in that one moment
the whole sky bottom
breathes and we
under gold blown
clouds are caught;
in–
haled again
we in that
catch of air
are there
with the wind
blown and
glowing
silent then
when the wind rushes
when it
breathes and blows.

Turning the Edge

Go out in the morning.
Cross to the next,
the great, valley, squinting
in the unexpected
crosslight. Both ridges
have been lumbered, plowed,
planted with houses or
let run to second growth.
Go, cut saplings,
build a raft, float it
down the James. Drown
your ax, the blade's marred.
Approaching the gorge
(it is afternoon now)
you cross corrugated shadows
of young trees.
                    The rapids: now
hold to the pressure,
the turning edge.

Evening at Lake Huron

The moon will turn full
and no further.
Beneath the black spruce
of Canada, granite,
the Grand Shield,
floats upon fire.
The birches' roots twist.
Deer dance for their tribe
free as the magma
that rises and dies.
Ten minutes' watch:
a striped skunk grubs ants,
breaking her fast.
Her small-fingered hands
work like the continents.

Bone Flute

And Pan did after Syrinx speed,
Not as a nymph, but for a reed.
  —Andrew Marvell, "The Garden"

1.

Look at this stone here:
grains of red
caught cold in gray.
A fire burns up
the ladder of the spine.
I've an old bone flute.
I play.

2.

The mind makes music
where water stands
inches deep on the thawing earth.
My heels drum.
My pulse knows the tune:
La, rings of birches!
Willow buds yellow.
Light on the river, the opening ice—

3.

Sharp and sweet
day touches the tongue.
Over the white mist
where creek's mouth hums

listen!
The breathing,
the swell of their wings.

4.

Marmot whistle—
At the ford, caribou
shoulder together.
Mauve airs eddy
round dun-furred horns.
Riverrock tremulo
to the meltwater's tune.
Playing harp: *the heart*
oh, I never thought
to make that thing.
And on I sing.

5.

Checking the traplines.
Small cymbals ring
from my fingertips.
Alone, I shade
the window and dance
to the moving light
of the single lamp.

Biosphere: Learning the Land

1. The Forest

October clouds are high, ice.
From a crest, I trace
the creeks down there
by sycamores' bones.
Here, chestnut ghosts
keep grubs and eggs
and rattling flickers
in their hollow hearts.
This is snake country,
sloping, rocky.
None today coil in the sun.
Darkness streams
from the zenith to push
the last light, turquoise,
to the basin's edge.

2. The Air

The white and gay
feathers of birds
grow out thin, horn covered,
then, dry, split the sheath.
In molting time,
primaries, down,
the short wing coverts,
drop silent,
marking the flyways,
thickest
at the points and capes.

3. The Sea

I watch for the Portuguese
men-o'-war, hanging households
of eaters and feelers,
birthers, stingers,
under bladders of air.
Anemones, others
of that family wave,
saintly, glowing
with radial symmetry.
Some kin produce
(though fixed themselves)
children: loose, free-swimming,
sexual medusae.
It cools. Beneath me
the long rays stop,
reds, yellow, green,
and all the light's blue.
In the depths it is
unseen, believed in, alluring,
ultraviolet.

Log: Our Position at Sunset

We cannot explain these,
or even try,
these great chunks of reality,
these dark evening cumuli.

The sight of a plane crossing,
smaller than a flight of starlings,
and silent, does not help us.
Nor can we doubt:
they are, rose and indigo, there.

A Natural History of Pittsburgh

1.

The duck falcon hunts Fifth Street.
Over flat, pebbled roofs
where the nighthawk's eggs lie,
chimney.swifts mount up,
chittering in the Pittsburgh dawn.

2.

This play of color in the skin
may continue for several hours
after the death of the cephalopod.
—B. H. *McConnaughey,* Introduction to Marine Biology

What rare shades!
Mount Washington is a nautilus.
The city, a squid,
secretive, benthic,
distracting predators, prey,
with its sepia ink.

3.

The Golden Triangle
is not what you think it is.

4.

Walk quietly through the streets of suburban Pittsburgh.
It is so late
that only the bathrooms are awake.

5.

1770: Twenty cabins surround the trading post.
Brown leaves on the hillsides
glow in the long sun.
Ore bewitches the compass.
Monongahela, Allegheny, Ohio,
the rivers fork like a dowsing rod.

6.

In winter it appears to be
a daguerreotype of itself.

7.

The life of the glacier is one eternal grind.
    —Encyclopedia Americana
The people of Pittsburgh rarely consider this.

8.

Around her neck,
like a saint's medal, Pittsburgh
wears the lava of her mills.

9.

The young queen ant,
royally fed,
is led to the surface and flies.
Come down from the bright air,
she pulls off her wings,
leaves them near the small males,
and goes to begin
a new city, underground, in the dark.

Alchemist's Notebook

We understand by "dazzling" two things: (a) the appearance of a strong source of light in the field of view, resulting in the other parts of the field being no longer clearly observable and (b) a feeling of giddiness or of pain.
   —M. Minnaert, The Nature of Light and Color in the Open Air

1. January: Meteor Storm

Last night the Quadrantid's stream
fell near the Dragon's head.
They left orbit, poured
in a downward arc to strike our air.
The stone turned to fire, a rain
from over the firmament.

I remember a tale
from the old time, when
the glaciers burned their round way south,
how Unavnuk's song filled her lungs.
A ball of flame hit and broke.
It shot inside her;
she ran to the igloo,
enthusiastic, and sang:
        "The great sea
        Moves me!
        The great sea
        Sets me adrift!

It moves me
Like algae on stone
In running brook water.
The vault of heaven
Moves me!
The mighty weather
Storms through my soul.
It tears me with it,
And I tremble with joy."
Her song was meat and blubber,
each time she sang, to those who heard.

2.   February: The Waters

Greater than orogeny is the rising up of spring.
Once I knelt by a snowdrop
whose fiery bud had made water of snow,
to bloom in an airy globe
under the icy crust. Now
the snow's dissolved. The rains have come.
The well is up.
The trees' net sucks and spits
into the sun's one eye. Water knows
no other way.
It rushes. It abides.

3.   March: Eclipse

Birds are small and far away,
fat in their nests. The sun shrinks.
Each twig is shadowed sharply, blued.
Is there no hole for us?
I gasp. I am drowning in air.
The sun shrinks. I squat by the mud.
Dark bands, the air's shades in level light,
race before wind. The distance burns.
I turn a stone, find a salamander,
amphibian of breath and flame.
It whispers in our common tongue:
        You must wait the wait.

Something will come.
After the water,
After the earth,
After the darkness, which is a sign.

4.   April: Sulphur Shower

Wind lifts the pollen. We talk of the ocean.
Roofs, paths, slow haired forearms, turn
sulphur green. Nights, we wake to drift together
on waves from the trees and are preserved.

Arthur Barlowe sailed that shore
"and smellt so sweet and so strong a smel,
as if we'd bene in . . . some delicate garden,
. . . by which we were assured, . . .
the land could not be farre."
It was the smell of the forest,
half of the continent swaying like censers.

5.   May: The Mountain

Today I ran down Tinker Mountain,
arms spun from my spine,
my faith in my feet,
the wheel's mark on my soles and palms.
At a spring, I drank,
let water fall from the dipper,
a hand on the forebrow.
The green ray flared up,
"the living light" from the setting sun.
Scots say, now I've seen it,
my heart will never err.

6.   June: Bioluminescence

Sixth month, time of longest light.
The fireflies flash yellow flash
green here by the stream flash orange,
wing through the thick air and mate.
They illumine a whole world.

On the Chao Phraya River they gather;
each leaf on each mangrove burns
and is cold and burns and is cold again,
for generations, for months.
Fests near Kyōto celebrate
their birth from the dry summer grass.
In New Zealand, glowworms suspend themselves
from the roofs of caves by silken sheaths,
luring gnats with their bluish green.
In the oceans, the sea phosphor and rotting wood,
corals, squid, and ocean worms shine.
Even in the abyssal zones where all the rays
seem dark, some gleam—
the peerers, gropers, gulpers of the deep.

7.   July: Butterflies

All afternoon I stayed in the slow
shades and yellows of the dusty house.
There, bottled and pinned, I found
a great spangled fritillary, its orange wings
washed gray and silver underneath.
The smells of butterflies are their true names:
the grayling's sandalwood;
the clouded yellow, heliotrope.
Some, white to our eyes,
wear color past violet,
markings unseen through any glass,
tints we never can know.

8.   August: Fire in Jerusalem

Across Kidron, the sun rose;
the city was made gold.
It has burned too long now.
Earth drinks the heat.
This is the place where David leapt.
Bold, near naked, he "danced
before the Ark
with all his might." His anger
sizzled away like the fat of an ox.

The Lord is with us!
Make merry with song!
The Lord is with us!
Make merry with lyres!
Make merry, make merry,
With tambour and cymbals!

These stones were Herod's.
I touch them, throat dry.
Soon the Khamsin will come, fifty days
of wind from the desert,
to quench our thirst with hot breath and dust.

9.   September: On the Ocean

The algae bloom
and stain the sea.
To cut the glare, I look
with half-closed eyes,
till shapes are only
light and shade.
Second equinox: dark balances day.
The water's gone red;
thunder rolls round the sun.
And still the earth heaves
and shoots out rock,
and the crumblings are scraped
and washed away.

10.   October: The Lost Land

Full autumn: night harvests.
In the long evening they told of him,
Prester John, who ruled—somewhere—
beyond Arabia, Thebes, under the southern sky's cross,
beside a spring in Maumet's sands.
He brushed the silence with visible wind.
He was threshed, and airy as chaff.
In these days he is lost, legend lost,
all lost save the ache of oak flails,
and gruel from the few grains
gleaned from a fireless earth.

11.   November: The Heiligenshein, or "Glory"

"The glory can be seen
by each one round his own head only."
Hoarfrost decks the grass.
Its lenses throw light
round my shadow's head, white
as the boreal water-sky
that reflects the far sea
and roofs earth with rime.
I could breathe now the currents
of the world's watery lung,
ocean's upwelling and sinking,
brightened phosphor at night.
Take the meal: protein,
and bread, and the Ghost's marbled fat.
I will not. The sea
is no fire. Light burns down.
And we must steer by the windward course,
until we are harbored all.

12.   December: Solstice

This, then, is the most dark, the *mørketiden*.
The clouds hang. Three days
since I've seen sun. I dreamed:
climbing, I came to the chambered root
of the ice river, knife slit
in the hot frozen flow.

Once we moved up the Great Rift,
our campfires a slow torch,
ash left for the apes
to wonder, or mock,
the bones for the wild dogs
whose eyes hung in air.
      Sisters, brothers, the hollow logs cry for us.
      Now we have taken leave, now we walk high.
      Sisters, brothers, it is lonely for us.
      Only the jackals catch our fire in their eyes.

This returning is a sign for the way.
I waken, and know these gifts: a world
molten, spun-off; birth in the sea;
a first in-breathing;
and the coming to earth. What turnings!
I have reached the crevasses, must pass down
beyond. Vi *går mot solen,* we go to the sun.

2
Cold Season

———◆◆◆———

The spirits were to be summoned with fresh words; worn-out songs could never be used when men and women danced and sang in homage to the great beast . . . all lamps had to be put out. Darkness and stillness were to reign in the festival house. . . . In deep silence they sat in the dark, thinking. . . .

It was this stillness we called qarrtsiluni, which means that one waits for something to burst.
—Mayuark of Little Diomede Island, on the Eskimo festival for the soul of the whale

Deer Yard

Voyces that seem to shine
For what else cleares the skie?
Tunes we can hear, but not the Singer see . . .
—*"The Sheepheards Song,"* England's Helicon

The winds have stilled.
All things wait for the snow.
Deer will gather, the same yards,

will pack thin trails,
leave iced depressions
where they've slept.

We find these and think
of necks stretched for cedar bark
as for sounds past the audible,

no new trails broken,
the trees stripped bare.
So we walk out in the wintertime,

search for tracks in the fresh falls,
trust only our eyes,
not the clear, ringing air.

Drifts pile up.
Clouds close round the sun.
We flounder and break through the crust, for hours.

Wind from the North

There is a longing comes to us,
not in the small hours
that are long, or at evening,
but in the noon's glare,
when wind crosses the snow.

Labrador, it may call,
racing the heart's beat,
or it may move slow
as Atlantic's deep current
that now near Antarctica
wells up, having sunk
in the far north seven hundred years past.

It does not know our fear:
the cooling of fires in the mountains' heart.
It is ice made blue
with new snow layers' weight.
As the yolk shrinks,
there's a move toward the shell.
We fall into the world.
There is a longing
that comes to us.

Northeast Passage

I woke to dream
in the far north, judged,
sent to pack ice, caught
by the northeast wind.

The dogs howl. We cross the ice
easing the sledge
at hummock and ridge.
The dogs eat their pups.
Tomorrow,
Johansen shoots my team, I his.
The bullets crack.
Leads split into the ice.

I sail with martyred Bering,
weeks in a white pitching room.
The floes jam, curse
the shifting yards.
I cry, a cub; cold
seeps under my soles.

One by one we lost them:
starved, coughing, dropping glare-blind
into the low sea, faces turned
away in the mute dark.
Finally, only the cook and the steward are left,
the cook, the steward, and Chinese Bok,
dead from the knees on down.

The sky's swollen—
still on the trail.
All day the heart
cuts a wake of snow
beneath the hovering wet-beaked sun.

December, Tombstone Cemetery, Roanoke

Now, the nights lengthen,
catching at ankles
like half-frozen soil.
Baneberry, creeper,
sprung up to meet you.
The last oak leaves rustle:
Go down, and, Go down.
Heat bleeds from your feet.

Snow,
if you should lie on your back,
will be seen black underneath
will be seen black as it falls
will show its absence of color
when you stare at the glow of the featureless sky.

There is, too, that quick catch,
the breath's,
when the moon breaks through.
The hair rises,
earth between graves.

Here in This Cellar

Here in this cellar
we've come to live.
Our bodies knot.
I quake for your hollow
whirling bones.
The pipes ring. In corners,
cold webs spin and
our whole world groans.
I mutter, Lord,
let us be salamanders
caught up in your flames.
Cast us to earth.
Grind us to bread.

Meditation on Fog and Fire

I'm cold. I don't know what word
I can send to you now:
something about bones ablaze
the day the fog came in.

What a thing to waken to! At times,
I'd rather you were huddled here,
our breaths kindling their own fog,
our bones secured and sunk.

I'd rather we were in Tierra del Fuego,
coughing, without any fire.
But my message: the flesh
is a fog that burns.
The fog is fire enough, rising,
to bring us round to cold.

Passing the Night

What end is there to the sorrow of graves?
—Mutammin ben Nuwaira

After noon, the flurries
finally stuck, flake blotting flake,
the asphalt stained white.
Dark drained into the sky,
slicked horizons, oozed west.
We go down to the city,
like boarding a scow,
talk not of death, but remembrance.
We edge into the crowd.

This is the wrong light:
inert gasses, mercury,
arced, wired, and shot.
Shot. I've heard, dying too quickly
one hovers for hours,
unaware of the passage.
Am I dreaming, I ask you—
this orange, hazy sky?
an undersea tunnel,
these tangled lanes?

Midnight. The rat hours.
Brush past the shufflers
rapt in caves of their sweat.
Lover, you whisper,
gaze fixed ahead, netted,

moth to a beam
that shines years through the air.
Red light. The dockyards.
Lost—this uncuttable
knot of cement.

We pass Dennis Imoto's
First-Rate Tatoo Shop.
Pain and love catch us up.
"To understand" is
"to divide," *ne?*
The city snarls.
Cars quarrel.
Trucks roll by, west,
deep into night's cone.

So dawn's come. Red
streets map your eyes.
Water runs—this hour—bright.
Sparrows wheel up in hunger.
You circle in grief.
Each day's river's new;
channels shift, bars
pile up, wash out. Someday
we may grasp this.
I hold you. Forms
sweep past. A watchcry:
"All, all, all
is well."

3
Correspondences

———•◦•———

. . . a metaphor is not a literary device but an actual meaning arising from, operating in and leading us to realize the co-inherence of being in being . . . we perceive forms because there are correspondences.

—Robert Duncan

Poem Written on a Windy Day in Iowa

1.

Before daybreak the wind rose.
I turn off my lamp at the first light;
outside the window, cedars hurl themselves
again and again at the face of the sun.

2.

This air out of Nebraska's night
is the cry of an old woman dying of joy,
heard only dimly here, in houses
crouched near the Father of Waters at dawn.

3.

We are no longer mourning the dead.
Alive, bodily fissures aglow,
we have come to a certain knowledge:
they spin around us still.

The Body Speaks

1.

For years I've been your grub,
your white slug.
You remarked my resemblance
to a foetal ape, and pondered,
and I stepped out
into the days.

2.

Haven't you seen?
The tones of your flesh:
the thighs, a bit yellow,
like melons,
the belly, orange,
the long spine violet,
the line of the torso white,
shot blue the breasts and rose
the curving backs of your arms.

3.

Lie in the tub. Look again.
Pearls fall in ropes
as hands glide up.
Feet are sly carp,
at rest now, eyeing
what drifts down their way.
Volcanic islands:
knees break the surface.

Above them, bowed,
twins right and left handed,
cradles, coves,
the old and new moons.

4.

I am no chrysalis
to hold will and soul.
I risk; I am both.
I am the butterfly.
Wet-winged now
I pull air
through my spiracles,
force blood to the pads,
let membranes stretch.
I harden.
I will fly.

After the Rains

After the rains,
clearing. Our first sight:
the moon hooks its tail

as if nothing had changed.
Four weeks of rain
come to an end. How many times

have I wakened beside you?
I remember I smashed
all my mirrors, cut moorings,

moved in. I forget all the rest.
What's left to us?
Silt clogs the spillways,

the dam roars, young willows
choke on the floodplain.
We fling on our coats,

rush, wordless; the lake
presses and presses the flank of the marsh.
Mists rise from new pools,

slip their arms round our waists,
murmur promises, plead with us,
stroke our faces, coax smiles.

Under the spruces, we lose the moon.
The trail turns. You vanish, ahead.
Deep in the woods, I look back and see

a long unknown figure
speeding white, flickering
in dim light past thin trunks.

Letter from the Provinces

The moon cuts into the room on horseback.
Sixty years ago
it was a lamp.
The dikes weaken yearly.
Spring's floods will swell.

This inkstick was father's.
I no longer remember
who owned the stone.

No matter. Insects hush.
The household prepares.
The winter plum blooms
in the Mongolian wind.

Tomorrow, the last time,
I'll go out the gate,
watch charcoal women
cut leafless wood.
I tell you, what little
we have is enough.

Elm Leaves

Elm leaves. Not curled oak,
or sycamore, broad
manuscript pages,

lapped over lap.
No, elm leaves, their jagg'd
asymmetrical shapes in-

dividual forms
flat on the earth,
like hands, fingers closed,

placed palm onto palm.
Hands on the earth:
yours pressed on mine,

your life thick
with sadness, leaves
heaped in a corner.

—Yes, but what kind?
Stretch out your hand,
clasp the leaves to your flesh,

pick out their scents:
vinegar, semen,
dust sun-warmed and wet,

apples, old metal—Do
you hear what I'm saying?
Take the leaves for your lover,

learn all their secrets,
wrap their veins round your fingers,
taste them, this world's own

particular beauties.

Mango Poem

1.

One mango
is a belly bearing the world.

2.

Cut with a stainless
steel cleaver, the slices
are irregular phases
of a crazy moon.
The flesh is peachlike and smooth,
riddled with fibers
forming an interface
next to the skin.

3.

Held to the cheek
they yield the scent
of a longing nearly satisfied.

4.

The seed:
ovoid, suprisingly flat,
two-thirds the fruit's length,
in color, chalk, a cuttlebone.
The sweetest flesh is clinging here.

5.

Now it happens, the thing you feared.
What you notice is
the sun's mango light
cast from the fruit to the whitewashed wall.

6.

Game for the eighth month:
float your lover a candle
in a red-dappled boat
of mango peel.

7.

In the market,
even at noon,
they are cool.
Without such things,
we are lost,
we are lost.

Consider

(after reading Chang Chi's "Night Mooring at Maple Bridge")

. . . or how the snail
in her whorled, agate shell
leaves a pure arc pared
off the moon's thready disc.
With such a rope, yes,
you could moor on the river
and sleep through the watchcries,
amid fisherfires, sleep,
while your boat waves, a slow foot,
under night maples, when
even the moon's gone
and the black birds cry once
and you rise to move, leaving
your single slick trail.

Poem Beginning with a Line by T'ao Ch'ien

"The weather's turned; I wake to time's change."
Last night, rain, after months of snow.
The room lit white. What? Lightning,
I realized, and hove under covers
like thunderhead banks. Spring's fallen.
The cold's blurring out. Warmth gathers,
moss blue green on stones where water falls,
free after months cloaked by frozen clouds.
The heat will come down, then leaves, until
the sun sets early, its angle declines,
and the dew fades from prism to autumn white.
Chill. Echoes. Chrysanthemum month.
The winter sacrifice, and days stretch out.
We'll pull into our clothes then, draw
comforts from shadows, strum mournful modes,
be strong when we can, you and I,
old T'ao, and raise cups together.

Imitating the Artist, or Her Story

1.

Web-weaver, Philomel,
her shuttle coursed right
and then left, an ox at the plow,
music its master, its sex cut away,
treacherous, steady, alpha
and beta back and forth on a page.

2.

Untongued, she gave voice
to her history,
stitched his crude rhapsody,
made swords of her skeins.
She sang the unspeakable
in after years—now
the words of the wordless
quiver still on the boughs
that loom here in words.

3.

And of her pain?
Song's scattered, the web,
a crumbled wall.
My throat burns, a daughter's.
This room, the mid-seventies—
warp and woof shake
to resounding waves:
our language, its artless
genesis, rape.

To the Reader

What do you ask of me?
I am the asp you clutch to your breast.
I breathed my last long ago,
ripe body rolled down under the clay.
I slide in the swollen side of a woman,
hysterical snake,
to make fresh my passage back to the world.
Tear open her flesh.
Grope through her guts.
There. Ah! No. *Slip*pery bastard!
Ignore me. I'll cut capers, naked,
you wouldn't believe.
Believe me and—sst!—
I'll close tight as a clam.
Climb. I'm an oak tree,
old as the hills, roots rotting away,
boughs thick with mistletoe, yes,
kisses of death.
I'm the light of the world but
lost in my forest
you can't see the *t*'s.
So it's finally that simple
once you set it all down
in lead black and white,
if you would just ask.

4
Maps

———◀•▶———

Heaven is so far of the Mind
That were the mind dissolved—
The Site—of it—by Architect
Could not again be proved—
        —Emily Dickinson

Poetry is the game we play with reality; and it is the game and
the play—the game by history and training, the play by instinct
and need—which make it possible to catch hold of reality at all.
        —R. P. Blackmur

Badakhshān, North of the Hindu Kush
(after Bill Byrd)

Already, fields of snow to the south. Long valleys finger into the hills, searching out a particular vein.

Word first came in the market. There, among baskets of cumin and apples, a bold wife hissed, flashed red hair, and vanished. The stall's nubbed coats turned to poplars in the wind.

The Shrine of the Heratic Sage. Around the sepulchure, verses brushed from the Book. In the village, sung, poems of lost love and deception, poems of destinies, of half-hidden signs.

Walking out. Steady rain, leaf onto leaf rotting, the sun lost for days. Near the delta's tangled, motionless pools shines a heap of white, polished stones.

Sitting in a teahouse, I am offered a walnut, soft and oily, unlike any other that I have eaten.

Lorain, Ohio

The YMCA in Lorain is built of old brick the color of shed blood. Drive in at dawn past the mills, the Ejército de Salvación, and the Tabernacle of God: ten thousand years since the glaciers left these beaches. Night-shift workers talk, low-voiced, in cafés. They and their children go on Sundays to the park where the great metal Easter basket stands, head-high and empty till the tulips rise. At Whitsuntide it will pour out geraniums. Now the first full sunlight strikes a column of smoke over the Black River Lumber Company. It is half-cloud, half-fire. Thin frost glitters, the frost on the trees in the holy city of Lorain, Ohio.

Advent: Driving South from Ohio

It is because we burn that we require the light.
                                        —*William Law*

The great sun when it's first up throws down its own shape,
coppers of light through the oaks' last leaves. The earth rolls and
flattens as we turn south, at the start of the year's shortest day.
Caught in the bottomlands, fog blurs the white fields, the brown
living woods. They've planted yews and cedars on new-cut slopes
that channel the interstate; icicles grip the rocks' shaded sides. Even
now, each shadow's sharp as a blade. Someone remembers the
sun's rays don't diverge: for us on this small world they strike as if
parallel. I hear this and drive, with a furious heart, in an orbit of
brightness, as though this road might lead to Damascus.

Stone of Heraclea

*In like manner, the Muse first of all inspires men herself; and from
these inspired persons a chain of other persons is suspended, who take
the inspiration.*

—*Plato,* Ion

The long sinks of geologic time, the mind's moves in memory and
imagination: the unreal and the no longer real the same as they pass
off the scale of the comprehensible.

We spin in the past. The earth itself is the wandering pole that
draws our needles. The frost-wedged ridges' shoulders heave, heap,
waste into talus, and head for the coast. Rivers fall, stone shifts, the
slow-breathing flexure of crust gives compass. And what now you
are in me, ten years lost, charges my life.

Once, now, still you climb the shadowed, shattering stairs in a
bombed-out opera house, long before carved with its epitaph, *Dem
Wahren, Schönen, Guten.* In it, things you stitched into story: rub-
ble-mountains gapped by water, Nebuchadnezzar's throne, masks
of the sun, dusting velvet, savannas, must, the falling light, your
young back's wings, this bounded declining universe, and snapped
there by its field, myself.

Conversation

Hours before dawn, there was rain. Now, your voice, and the last lashes of wind. We have let the darkness settle again, flakes drifted in corners of a trapper's shack. Outside sweeps a forest of firs, and snow, old friend, deep in the sun! Within, a cold dust sifts through the chinks. By the chimney, he mutters, stroking his pelts. You and I fall silent, nothing to say. Waterless flurries, traps freezing shut, the dry breath of the old man—we bear these things, this world, were born to.

February Thaw

We have wrapped ourselves round with hollows of air, a winter of breath, in cold, clear light. Noon: long blue shadows flee before us; we pursue. There, you tell me, there is the house where I lived with her, see that window, the moon climbed its small panes. Ice in the valley creaks. Pale roots from the eaves drop seeds of water on fallow soil. Something under us whirls. Memories condense and sink, burrowing down to rest at last. For the first time our voices meet, waves reflected from the snow of high peaks, come back to us now as spring turns, as the light wells, as the river opens, rising to flood.

Alba Written after the War Ends

"The war is dead," you tell me. I hang a watch on a gold chain, to lie between my breasts. Initials, my grandmother's, writhe on the case, leaves in a jungle on fire. It is time that you left. The rivers and villages in me belong to the enemy; gather your honor, your ignominy, and depart. The curtains shake in the first pulses of daylight. Somewhere a whore weeps for a soldier. Young men wander the alleys, crying their victory, staring with wonder at the guns in their hands. The war is dead. It has gone underground, waits; its chancres will burst near our mouths. We plunge into the grass at the edge of a radar screen, hoping to leave no trace. Now the birds moan, we've had what we wanted, our clothes lie in heaps, possessed and discarded. Blue flames, unstoppable, lick the edge of the rug.

Mushroom

Only just May; already we think of the summer. Horse chestnut leaves grown full-sized in five days, the jonquils going, scattered maples the deep red that chlorophyll masks from spring to October. I've looked you up because someone mentioned Hiroshima and death makes me horny. But behind your kitchen a cherry tree explodes into bloom like a bad joke. Forget it, I've got a headache, my period's coming, there are shadows of bodies burned on the wall there, I can't even see you. The glare.

Definition: Ch'ing

1. In the first picture, a simple rural landscape somewhere
on the old silt of the Great Plains. It is midwinter; no individual
cloud can be distinguished, but the whole sky is theirs. The white
frame house, the graying barn, the two sheds in the middle dis-
tance, are outlined in half-melted snow. It is in this season that they
reveal their wooden affinity for the few trees in the yard. The rest of
the scene, except for the curving strip of poplars and willows where
an iced-over stream has cut through the soil, is fields, furrows
marked with white on the northern face.

At the horizon, there is a dark form, a woodlot, that becomes
a backdrop upon the sudden appearance of a feather floating down-
ward, brilliant, kingfisher blue.

2. Here, a portrait of one of the shorter-lived emperors of
the Han dynasty, more precisely, of the Later Han, after the revi-
talizing reign of Wang Mang. The eyes rest always at a point be-
yond the observer; the skin is creamy, flawless. Only the thinnest
layer of fat smooths over the cheekbones and jaw. He wears a
scholar's plain gown.

He was buried, though, in robes embroidered with a crane,
some bamboo leaves, dragons. And on his tongue, for all these
centuries, he has held a disc of polished, blue-green jade.

3. This mountain takes its name from our subject. It was
caught on a singularly bright day, so that the steely outcrops of
granite reflect not only the sun's light, but blue tones from the sky
itself. Conifers cover the faces of this great heap; a similar light is
shot from their new-tipped branches.

But around their trunks, and on the shadowed slopes, they
sink through deeper shades, toward indigo, and black.

4.   After crossing the paddy fields in the month when they turn from muddy pools to stands of yellowing rice, at the hour when the flickering of dragonflies yields to the melody and counterpoint of summer frogs, we find, pushing back the foliage, this view of a cave. The rocks at the entrance catch the last glow of the turquoise west; their lichens paint them lapis lazuli.

Stay a moment on the threshold, absorbed and still, like a wading heron. Within, perhaps, is the lair of a black fox, or heaps of sapphires and sealstones, some child's lead horse, histories on bamboo slips, artifacts of tin and bronze. Within, (one grows certain) lies none of these things, or all, or the quality that unites them.

5.   On my desk, as it is represented here, stand a basket of green plums and a light infusion of tea. For what purpose was this assemblage begun? A synthesis, a capturing? Fragments of other pictures litter the surface: the sign from a wineshop or brothel, mosses, a wound blue at the edges, several copper pennies.

Inside the brilliant cup of the lamplight, the viewer catches at last a reflecting eye, dark at the pupil, the iris a pale bluish gray, and (visible only to the most perceptive) traces of some form of color blindness, amaurosis, a gradual decay of the sight.

Ch'ing:

青   The color of nature;
green, blue, black. A
drab, neutral tint.
—*Mathews' Chinese-English Dictionary*

5

Voyages

———◆●◆———

Language and myth stand in an original and indissoluble correlation with one another, from which they both emerge but gradually as independent elements. They are two diverse shoots from the same parent stem, the same impulse of symbolic formulation, springing from the same basic mental activity, a concentration and heightening of simple sensory experience. In the vocables of speech and in primitive mythic figurations, the same inner process finds its consummation: they are both resolutions of an inner tension, the representation of subjective impulses and excitations in definite objective forms and figures.

—Ernst Cassirer

So, on this dark winter's morning, when the real world has faded, let us see what the eye can do for us.

—Virginia Woolf

James Cook in Search of Terra Incognita

The Ship is rigged with Ice.
There is no Wind here, no sound
save the lapping of waves on dirty Icebergs,
the Crew's curses, the Complaints
of the Gentleman Scientists,
the Squeals of the farrowing Sow.
Gray-white Albatrosses
slip in and out of the Mist
and mark still the same Spot
where Neban Peters, Seaman A.B.,
flew from the Rigging and entered
the Sea. Should we find it,
we'll name the new Land for him.
But I fear that the Admiralty
will be sorely displeased:
no plunder, no trade, no glory for Empire,
or myself.
Is it Folly to seek out, to chart
the High Latitudes?
Then let it be well
and bravely done.
It is such Folly makes us
what we are.
Word comes from the Surgeon.
Despite his best efforts,
and those of the Cook,
the last Piglet has died of the Cold.

James Cook in Delirium

Is that a Bird in the room? I remember
the Land Birds, how they cheered us
as we drew near Australia. No,
this is Java, I am chill with Malaria,
I burn like the low Sun

the day my *Endeavour* wrecked
among Breakers league-long
at the Great Barrier Reef.
Where are my Charts?
I shall write in the names—

Point Hicks, New South Wales, Botany Bay,
good English names! Father
could farm that land, if he'd but leave
Yorkshire. Those Savages
daubed themselves white,

threw clumsy Boomerangs, Spears,
until my Marines fired over their Heads,
startling them back
to the Bush. And we took the Land.
What's this now? No Memory:

my own tall Figure face down in the Surf.
Strange blossoms. The Cries
of fleeing Brown Women,
the Birds' cries of the Women
as they faltered and ran.

The Japanese Poet Writes from America

Unbearable clarity. In this raw world
leaves burn out too soon.
Grand Tetons, the Great Plains:
a thousand *ri* of alien corn.
And the sky so blue today,
a long bow shot
by the snow's harsh beams.
Only at sunset, as darkness draws in,
I go down to the floodplain,
make peaks of the buildings
up on the banks,
and imagine that whole archipelago
of persimmon and gold
a half gleam, sunk in the mists
caught by sheltering precipices
that are not there.
Me? I could sleep for months
in the haze of my own moist air.
My eyes gather fog.
I return to the water's cut.
I am lightheaded, a river on fire.

Poem from Iona

It has even been suggested that the artist of one or more of the pages must have been near-sighted—for his work, a benign optical defect that was itself a magnifier.

—*Alfred Friendly on* The Book of Kells

The last mists gray
as the sun sifts through,
chaff angling down
onto winter's near stones.
Mole, I was called, and I cast up the earth.
Lord, leave my orb whole!
I am fond of my sight.
I prefer to thy light
this visible dark.
But the mists streamed around
and the peacock rolled out
its bright hundred eyes.
Page grimmaced to life:
lapis and spirals, the angels' twist,
billow of fire, a wingéd man,
lion, belovéd eagle, and ox.
I put down my words.
I take up my brush.
Let the lens seek its flaw
for sun's glory's sake.
I will be blind man;
God's fool I will be.

Driving toward Nebraska

Oskaloosa, Iowa, July first,
a hundred and five, under mackerel skies.
　—Look! Geyser plumes in the sorghum fields.
—No, rogue corn.
　—Or whales, a school out for play.
—Seed from the old crop.
　—Green herons. Earth's tongues.

And so we wrangle our way into town,
one house graced by a single stalk,
well past knee-high, shot up from a crack
in the walk—miracles! Born again,
all of us, soon.

Back east, the reservoir:
we drove slow as silt
past those gray wooden bones.
The bottomland's back,
a new forest springing,
child of the drought.
One thing we agreed upon,
our joy and our thirst.

Impatient, we've stopped
in a young orchard for shade.
I catch sight through the branches:
at last, unmistakable,
on the bluff, headstones.
They wax, unripe, lanterns
on the limbs of the trees.

Digging

The moon dawns voiceless
as surgical flint.
Even Africa moves, a tooth
in the old mouth of earth.
We stir our fire cold,
heap it with dirt,
and find in our sleep's
deepest stratum a troupe
of orangutans grease-painted,
chuckling and pushing,
proud to their spines.

Cut to:
a great orange figure
with ascetic's tits
cradling a hairless
thin-browed kid. She hands me a trowel.
I start to sift loess.
Somewhere to the east
is the great crescented block
of granite that—
        "THAT DOES NOT MOVE."
Who's there?
I, in a frenzy, move the earth,
several bucketsful.

Under the red moon
the potter's wheel spins.
She forces the clay.
I climb the *tel* toward her
mumbling of Jericho
aping the neolithic
soon to remember
the true tongue,
our old home.

An Anatomy

. . . *the eye sees nothing but the light of the sun.*
—*Marsilio Ficino,* de Amore

1.

What holds us together?
The whole head's weight
turns on its axis.
Organs hover in orbit
round the body's chained pole.
Six blind probes
of this sensitive pachyderm:

> hill ranges, landfill,
> a crumpled globe
> grown into itself

> wet, moon-struck spheres
> riddled by red

> webbed wings, bivalves,
> smithies within
> drumming deafening drums

> dumb dark twins
> hairs line these caves
> that bell with the nameless
> waves of the air

appetent, languid,
this rough, knowing snake

the last stops short,
trusting the sentries
that the borderland's honest
of this Deseret, Oz.

2.

And all the while
tides whisper about them.
In chortling chorus,
the joints guffaw.
Synapses snicker,
shot mad with the secret,
their images passing
drugged with belief
through the colorful galleries
knotted over the spine.
This is the place
of our unlearned knowledge.
Here, where our stars fell,
parts filled the soul's rents
padding the cells
that we knew before knowing,
filling the frame
that is known last of all.

The Last of the Glades Indians Ready Their Canoes

We have gathered our last things;
our mounds will remain and we
will go.
We are leaving the slow river, miles
of sawgrass spilled over marl.
We are leaving the hummocks,
the sloughs trembling with heat,
the deer that browse
bellies deep in the marsh
and start up like sparks when the panther nears.

What will that land have?
Not the seashoals
where racoons wade nights,
not the trails
of water braided
when mangroves catch land
and build at their roots.

Now the sun
rushes in from the west,
and the whole sky smokes with birds.
Soon we will leave,
perhaps without reason,
or for reasons no greater than cold coming down.
The first call of a night wailer flames
out of the evening hard at our backs.

Everglades Journal

```
  ── ──        ── ──
  ─────        ── ──
  ── ──        ─────
  ── ──        ─────
  ─────        ── ──
  ── ──        ─────
```

K'an: Li:
the abysmal,   *the clinging,*
water   *fire*

As water pours down from heaven, so fire flames up from earth.
While K'an means the soul shut within the body, Li stands for na-
ture in its radiance.

— *I Ching*, Wilhelm/Baynes translation

1.

Traveling inland, new charts;
gone from the warm green sea.

Then I was husk and jelly milk.
Now my canoe:
                the frame bleached bone
chalk-hard, riddled
like the deep-laid lime
skins stretched over
ligament-stitched (gleaming, dull)
sail set, out
on the yearlong flow.

There, where
the polyps swayed
near chambered colonies
veiled out in whorls
clumped on their long
dead, praying on
their own stone lace—
there, in the ocean
I danced to a tune
sweet as an apple
warm as a cow
      drumming like a lover's thrusts
      until the piper plucked me up
named his ransom
set me south.

2.

What is this grace
to which I have fallen?

Listen!
      a river
fifty miles from bank to bank
half a mile an hour it moves
south by sou'west
through sawgrass glades.
By the river's want I set my course
by shafts of water
the nerves' sparks' net.
My body, now, is pricked and pumped
the heart stung quick
its lamp afire.

In the Everglades
the fat soil burns
for three months, four
and the rains come up
and the ash goes down

and the ash goes down

in the maw of the earth
and in early day, the heron's out.
Her fine neck quivers, gone in the hunt

and one in her are scanner, screen—
scanner and screen and charging field.

3.

Aloft on the swift wind
running out the storm
in threes and tens the birds rise up
to rush headlong for the marbled east.

I bring down sail.
I drift toward the west.
The hard-beat rain off the far gray gulf
drums us all down
when it gathers us round:

the blue heron, the great white
roseate spoonbills
ospreys and egrets
the vulture, the watcher
the diving anhinga that plunges in pools
and, brighter hours, spreads wide his wings
a feathered cross, to dry in the sun.

Now near the storm's grasp
a kingfisher calls.
> *Wait for the Jordan wind*
> *the weather-change wind*
> *the wind from the sea.*
> *The wind shards cut your fat away.*
> *The wind will set you free.*

4.

Arrow evil, the slight gar
hangs in the water
sharp as a heart.

Winter
dry
the earth's skin cracks.
The gar gasps, lost
out of water's globe
as I if on wax wings
risen too far
would die while my blood boiled
in the moon's dark ring.

So soon my pulse simmers:
a shape hoves out

out of the winter mud into the last pool.
The gar goes down to that piper's tune.

> *lord of the long fast*
> *the boneyard, the river*
> *ruler of the wet and dry*
> *king of ash and fire*

5.

Have reached the river's woven mouth.

Over the brackish mangrove shoals
great flocks head home by the sun's rare red.
In nourishing marshes, pelicans
preen and prick their glossy breasts.
In rookeries laid on the salty isles
they dance for their unborn.

> *Their children are waiting.*
> *They wail in the wind.*
> *My children are flowers*
> *needles and shadows*
> *cast on the sea.*

And the late-day wind comes down
comes down
and the late-day wind
comes down:

You who let your heart first leap
who called your tune, and played, and pranced

you are the salt bone
the hover-out, the ash-gone gar.
You are the waving marsh
the beak, the blood, the gulf-born cloud.
Yours now the lost shore,
                              the glades of grass
the arrow flow, the husk that cracks
and the cells you wrapped
round that first wet fire.

Still the heart hungers
after the sea
the sea undivided
its breakers coiled
a light-shot line
on the carbon coast.
        Listen.
What is it?
        A shaft of fire
        veiled round with signs.
But night's bird's up.
Her blue wings banking,
she weeps and preys;
sings; drops;
trembles;
yields no quarter;
soars; pursues.

The Desire for Perpetual Prayer

Then forget all that.
While first you look
toward the east light, yes,
the land rolls out
at your feet, new-wet,
humped and puckered,
the river's work.
But you turn down
the shaded slope,
frost ruffling the plantain leaves,
into the cloud
on the unnamed lake.
(A stream dammed:
roots gasp their last;
waters divided
rise and are stilled.)
Two geese loom,
gray marked with white,
a beat in their throats:
lod-lod, lod-lod,
teach us the names.
And over your shoulder
haze too bright to bear.
Steam stirs up.
The surface shifts.
Track mink and muskrats
to the caldron's edge
and deep in it trace
the torn trees' runes
their twigs gone up,

and washed away,
like the dizzy words
of black-hatted men, sidelocks a-twirl.
So there you are,
with the fog and the sun
and a duller disc
on the water's face—
a wet moon, lengthening,
a lens of light,
an oval now,
a sword in flames.
It splits itself
and thousands dance
and you want to cut
your tongue away:
No graven things.
(A maze of letters
shifts on a wall.)
But image renounced,
what left? the phoneme
come to us trailing
clouds of glamour?
the numen? die Namen?
the thing itself
turned all to stone
and your head enwreathed?
cadence, your own voice,
die dürren Blätter,
Klang und nicht Sprache?
Choose:
charcoal tracings
under the oils,
or the woman's throbbing,
her salt-dry skin;
the silvered glass
that steals, or its shards,
broken brilliance
on watch in the dark.
Oremus.
        "Gelobet—"
Texts from the serpent's mouth,
or tongues of the wind.

About the Series

James Cook in Search of Terra Incognita is the fourth collection in this series established by Virginia Commonwealth University in 1975 and sponsored jointly by VCU, the Associated Writing Programs, and the University Press of Virginia. *James Cook* was selected from 457 collections solicited nationally by the editorial board of the Associated Writing Programs and read by twenty-one poets from throughout the country. Every manuscript was judged by two independent readers, and those collections that received two outstanding recommendations were given to a third reader. Only three collections received three outstanding recommendations, while six others were cited as excellent. All nine were then read by Robert Penn Warren, who selected *James Cook* as the superior collection, making it the only one to receive four outstanding votes. *James Cook* was edited by Walton Beacham, although the volume needed very little editorial assistance. The VCU Series for Contemporary Poetry publishes at least one collection every year, and manuscripts are invited in the fall through the Associated Writing Programs.

About the Poet

Born in Washington, D.C., in 1950, Jeanne Larsen grew up on army posts in Kansas, Virginia, Pennsylvania, and West Germany and has subsequently lived in many states, Israel, and Taiwan. She holds degrees from Oberlin College and Hollins College and is currently researching her Ph.D. dissertation—a study of the T'ang Dynasty Chinese poet Hsüeh T'ao and her literary predecessors—to complete her graduate studies at the University of Iowa. She lives in Nagasaki, Japan, with her husband, Tom Mesner, and her two stepchildren, Scot and Kili.